E E k

Pocketbook

By
Margaret Thorsborne
& David Vinegrad

Cartoons:
Phil Hailstone

Published by:

Teachers' Pocketbooks
Laurel House, Station Approach,
Alresford, Hampshire SO24 9JH, UK
Tel: +44 (0)1962 735573
Fax: +44 (0)1962 733637
Email: sales@teacherspocketbooks.co.uk
Website: www.teacherspocketbooks.co.uk

*Teachers' Pocketbooks is an imprint of
Management Pocketbooks Ltd.*

Series editor – Linda Edge.

All rights reserved. No part of this publication
may be reproduced, stored in a retrieval system
or transmitted in any form, or by any means,
electronic, mechanical, photocopying, recording
or otherwise, without the prior permission of
the publishers.

© Margaret Thorsborne & David Vinegrad 2009.

This edition published 2009.
Reprinted 2011, 2012, 2014, 2015.

ISBN: 978 1 906610 10 4
E-book ISBN: 978 1 908284 90 7

British Library Cataloguing-in-Publication
Data – A catalogue record for this book is
available from the British Library.

Design, typesetting and graphics by **efex Ltd**.
Printed in UK.

Contents

Foreword

In understanding why the word *justice* might have some bearing on the way a school manages its behaviour policy and practices, it's helpful to know some of the history of the *criminal* justice system as it stands today.

Our current criminal justice system regards crime as a violation against the state. It requires that someone is held accountable (found guilty) and sees the job of the state as administering a punishment that fits the crime.

Many schools adopt a parallel philosophy: when young people break the rules of the school, they must be held accountable and the school administers an appropriate punishment (often called 'consequence'). In both cases the sanctions have usually been decided in advance and the law books, legislation or school policies are consulted to choose the appropriate consequence.

Foreword

This approach to doing justice is relatively new in the history of mankind. It can be traced back to the Norman invasion of England in the 11th century.

In rising to the challenge of bringing peace to a country beset by civil strife, William the Conqueror declared wrongdoing/crime to be a 'disturbance of the King's peace'. In doing so, the King (and therefore the state) became the primary victim of the crime. The real victim's needs were ignored, and justice was administered by officials on behalf of the King/state.

The parallel in schools is obvious. Schools are mini 'states'. The 'officials' are the Headteacher or principal, the senior leadership team, the class teacher, and so on, each with varying degrees of authority to dispense suitable consequences.

Foreword

There is, however, a remarkable reform underway in the criminal justice system. Victims, after long being invisible, have found their voice. This has happened as more ancient practices (practices that place emphasis on restoring relationships and meeting people's needs in the wake of harmful incidents and wrongdoing) are being recovered.

'Restorative justice' is a broad term to describe an approach to managing crime and wrongdoing that can be traced back to First Nation people and indigenous communities prior to western settlement and colonisation. Historians find mention of 'restorative' practices as far back as 2000 BC.

Modern restorative justice began in the mid 1970s in Canada and the USA with victim-offender 'encounters'. Some countries initially adopted restorative justice programmes to divert young people from court and thereby avoiding the slippery slope into the criminal justice system and a life of crime. Schools are now getting in on the act.

Foreword

So how is this ancient restorative justice different from what we currently do?

It demands that we think about what happens to **the victim**, and how the victim's needs might be met in the aftermath of the crime/wrongdoing. It also requires us to consider the other stakeholders in the event and what their needs might be.

We can start by considering the **offender** or **wrongdoer**. Punishing the offender offers little in the way of genuine accountability; it does little to meet a victim's needs and little to address the causes of the wrongdoing. Punishment alone does not **make things right**; indeed it changes very little for the wrongdoer's circumstances.

The community, a major stakeholder in the effects of wrongdoing and crime, can rightly be regarded a secondary victim. But the community also has **responsibilities** – to victims, to wrongdoers and to itself. The saying '*it takes a whole village to raise a child*' is never more true than when we consider the role a school plays within a community in developing young people into responsible citizens. If we are to be clever with crime/wrongdoing, we must look to broader contributory issues.

Foreword

In an era when school disciplinary traditions surrounding the use of punitive sanctions no longer seem to deliver the desired outcomes, schools are rethinking their behaviour management philosophy and practices. Those that have adopted restorative principles are reporting:

- Better relationships with young people
- Greater engagement in learning
- Greater development of important social and emotional competence in learners

This Pocketbook is a practical guide to restorative practice in schools, based on the principles of restorative justice. It will show why restorative practice wins hands down as an approach to disciplinary matters and will enable you to get started with RP in your own school.

Introducing Restorative Practice

Relationships and Fair Process

Restorative Responses

The Restorative Continuum

The Small Group Conference

The Big Discipline Issues

Final Words of Advice

Introducing Restorative Practice

What is restorative practice?

Restorative practice (RP) is based on the philosophy and principles of restorative justice (RJ). Restorative practice involves:

- Viewing crime/wrongdoing through a 'relational' lens – understanding **that harm has been done** to people and relationships
- Understanding that when such harm is done, it creates **obligations and liabilities**
- Focusing on **repairing** the harm and **making things right**

How does it work?

This means that when things go wrong you:

- Involve those responsible for and those affected by the behaviour in solving the problem
- Provide high levels of support for all parties, whether perpetrators or those affected
- Address the needs of all those involved in harmful incidents
- Provide strong messages and reminders about what behaviours are acceptable and unacceptable

Your first reaction might be that no one has this sort of time to give! Be reassured that the investment of your time will reap dividends, including saving time in the long run. UK schools that have embarked on this journey report strong improvements in behaviour, ethos and academic outcomes.

RP is not a plug-in programme. It is a philosophy and a way of living and breathing school values. It requires whole school buy-in, high quality professional development and careful implementation.

Putting RP into practice – Sam and Kyle

Let's look at an incident that involves bullying behaviour and see how RP can guide your response:

It's break time, and you are just about to head to the staffroom for a cup of coffee when you witness an incident between two pupils. As students leave your classroom, Sam trips Kyle who stumbles to the floor. Kyle gets up and is then pushed against the display wall by Sam.

How should you deal with this incident?
What responses are available to you?

What happens next?

1. You could turn a blind eye and ignore or pretend you didn't see the incident because you're in a hurry to get to that cup of coffee.
2. You could see it as a bit of harmless 'boys will be boys' fun that, at best, would require a mild admonishment and save Sam from certain punishment if referred to the Deputy Head's office.
3. You could come down hard on Sam and dish out some strong medicine.
4. You could bring together the two boys involved and solve the problem in a way that is both respectful and constructive.

As teachers, how we manage an incident like this is important. We need to choose an approach that will deliver **useful** outcomes. We need to be aware of the **benefits and risks** for the students – and for us – in our choice of response. Above all, we need to be clear about our responsibilities and roles in shaping the social skills, character and emotional competence of the young people in our care.

We can explore the Sam and Kyle incident in more depth by comparing the four possible responses within the helpful framework of a 'Social Discipline Window'.

A Social Discipline Window

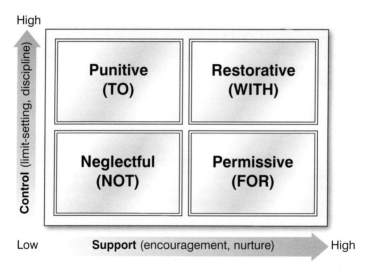

High

Control (limit-setting, discipline)

| Punitive (TO) | Restorative (WITH) |
| Neglectful (NOT) | Permissive (FOR) |

Low   **Support** (encouragement, nurture)   High

Social Discipline Window (Watchel, 1999) Used with permission

Using the Social Discipline Window

In the Social Discipline Window opposite, the horizontal axis represents the emphasis placed by the teacher or school on support for students – how you encourage and nurture them as learners and meet their individual needs as members of a school community.

The vertical axis is about structure and limits. It represents the emphasis placed by the teacher or school on the rules, boundaries and standards that are in place to provide the best possible environment for teaching and learning – how you manage the classroom learning environment, how people treat each other in that environment, and what the constraints and limits are for everybody's behaviour.

The way you respond to an incident might be seen as **neglectful, permissive, punitive** or **restorative**.

How do the four possible responses to the 'Sam tripping Kyle' story fit within this framework?

1. Neglectful – NOT holding students accountable

If you walk away and turn a blind eye you are being **neglectful**; you don't do anything about the problem.

In choosing to do nothing, you do **NOT** offer any support nor do you provide any reminders about behavioural limits and boundaries. You do **NOT** hold students accountable.

You risk sending mixed messages to students about what is important (valued) and what is expected. Students will not be able to trust you to keep them safe and may form the view that you don't care.

You choose not to use your authority.

2. Permissive – support FOR the wrongdoer

If you try to excuse or minimise the wrongdoer's behaviour (*'Sam is really an OK kid – he's just having a bad day'*) and the incident (*'Boys will be boys – it's just a bit of fun'*) with a mild admonishment, you are **permissive**. You may prefer not to make a fuss because it might risk your relationships with Sam and his friends. You may want to be liked.

Tut tut!

With this approach, you offer high levels of support **FOR** Sam (but not for Kyle, incidentally) with a low emphasis on reinforcement of expectations. You risk doing a disservice to wrongdoers by not confronting them with the impact of their behaviour, and victims feel as if you don't care enough about what they are going through.

You choose not to wield your authority appropriately.

3. Punitive – things done TO the students

If you come down hard on the wrongdoer by reprimanding loudly, criticising and/or applying a sanction to Sam with no constructive input from Kyle – the victim in this story – you are **punitive**.

By making this decision, you do things **TO** students. The emphasis is on the rule (about bullying, in this instance) and on Sam's non-compliance. He deserves to be punished because everyone knows what the predetermined sanction is for bullying. If you don't punish him, he will 'get away with it.' You impose high levels of limit-setting, usually by applying consequences.

However, you provide little or no support for either party and certainly invite no input from them. You risk humiliating wrongdoers and disempowering victims. Not only have you missed the opportunity to fix the rift in relationships, you risk wrongdoers 'losing face' with peers thus inviting payback to the victim later on.

You choose to take a top down authoritarian approach where non-compliance must be punished.

4. Restorative – things done WITH the students

If you bring together the students involved and create a space for respectful dialogue in which you act as facilitator, you are being **restorative**; you do things **WITH** students. With this approach you signal that the behaviour is unacceptable, but engage both parties in helping to sort out the problem constructively – ie high emphasis on meeting the parties' needs with fair process (support).

It's easy to think that you just don't have time to involve yourself in this style of problem solving, and be tempted to go for a quick fix. However, time spent using an effective and fair process is time well invested as the issues are unlikely to recur.

You choose to take an authoritative approach (making constructive use of your authority).

In conclusion

Returning to Sam and Kyle, the fourth option on page 13 best encapsulates the restorative philosophy in that it:

- Recognises that harm has been done and needs fixing
- Holds Sam (and possibly his friends) accountable
- Empowers Kyle and gives him a voice
- Exemplifies the value you place on healthy relationships between the key parties

The next section will explain why the restorative option with its emphasis on relationships and fair process is the most effective approach.

Introducing
Restorative
Practice

Relationships
and Fair
Process

Restorative
Responses

The
Restorative
Continuum

The Small
Group
Conference

The Big
Discipline
Issues

Final Words
of Advice

Relationships
and Fair Process

Some considerations

Why should relationships and fair process be given such prominence when it comes to managing pupils and behaviour? When we work with schools in the UK and elsewhere, we find it helpful in answering this to ask teachers to reflect on the following related questions. They stimulate robust debate and help to establish some common ground before introducing new concepts:

1. What is the purpose of 'discipline'?

2. What are we trying to teach our young people?

3. What do we believe about the role of the teacher in a young person's life?

4. What do we know now about the way the brain develops through childhood and adolescence and into adulthood?

5. What are the most effective ways to achieve long-term behaviour change? Is punishment effective?

6. Is it important to us that young people feel safe at school?

7. What is our role in the development of social and emotional competencies in learners?

8. How important is the relationship between teacher and learner, and how important are the relationships between learners?

Can we all agree on...?

Typically, the usual 'facts' that most workshop participants agree on in response to the previous questions include:

1. 'Discipline' is needed so that order prevails, enabling teaching and learning to happen with minimal disruption and maximum engagement.

2. It's important that young people experience consequences for flouting the rules or breaking the boundaries. (For most people this means punishment of some sort.)

3. Teachers have an influence (positive or negative) in the development of character and this is usually achieved through the quality of the relationship we have with the learner.

4. The brain is not fully developed until early adulthood; impulsive behaviour is common until then. The conversations that teachers have with young people, and the disciplinary responses, can significantly affect brain chemistry and the development of new neural pathways that will lead to new habits.

Can we all agree on...?

5. Self control and awareness of 'other' develops over time. Part of the purpose of school behaviour policy and practice is to assist that development. Punishment, although effective in achieving compliance in the short term, is not effective in developing independent thinkers and resilient learners, nor in engendering thoughtfulness and awareness of the impact of their behaviour on others.

6. Engagement in learning happens best when the learner feels safe with the teacher and other learners.

7. Social and emotional development is inextricably linked to how people relate to each other in the classroom and playground and is influenced by the intended curriculum and other supportive programmes. Modern education insists that teachers are primarily responsible for the social experiences of learners at school. Teachers cannot be seen as disconnected and distant figures in the classroom.

8. Quality relationships are among the most important elements in creating a productive and safe classroom where individual needs are met and a sense of 'community' is developed.

The power of relationships

What we know for sure is that the quality of the relationships among all members of a school community has a huge impact on safety, on learning and on teachers' professional satisfaction. When we challenge schools about their alignment of values with daily practice, we ask them to consider the following:

*'If you say that relationships matter, **to what extent** are relationships placed at the centre of your disciplinary philosophy and practice? If your answer is that they are 'very important', then perhaps the punitive philosophy that informs your practice may just be counterproductive.'*

If there is no process in place in schools to bring about healing and to restore relationships, the risk is that learners will remain stranded – alienated and disconnected from the class and, soon, from learning. The RJ philosophy places relationships at its core, and in the process perhaps it can maximise engagement and learning. But implementing it means learning to think differently, and the first stage is to ask: *'In the wake of an incident what **outcomes** are you after?'* The answer to this question will help you decide on the best strategy.

Outcomes vs strategies

While your responses to the Sam and Kyle story in the previous section may not be quite as clear cut as *not* doing anything, or doing things *to*, *for* or **with** pupils, it is crucial to look at how you think through the business of outcomes.

This will not necessarily be something you are used to doing, but it's a technique you need to train yourself into – it will help you to make good decisions and to focus on issues of fairness. The problem is that, as teachers, we tend to confuse **outcomes** with **strategies**.

For example, putting Sam in lunchtime detention is a strategy. But what do we want the detention strategy to achieve? Do we even know the answer to this question? If your answer is *'I want to teach Sam a lesson so that he doesn't do that again'*, then you are on the right track, but haven't gone quite far *enough* in your thinking!

We are so used to thinking that punishment is the only way to teach the lesson, we forget to think about exactly what lesson we want Sam to learn!

Deciding outcomes

So when you tackle an incident like the one Sam and Kyle have been involved in, start by identifying the outcomes you're hoping for. Use the following questions for guidance:

1. **Who are the people you need to consider** in terms of these outcomes? (The victims, the wrongdoers, the bystanders, the teachers, the parents, the organisation.)

2. **What do you want for each of them?** (That they are reassured, feel safe, have materials replaced, meet obligations, take responsibility, learn from the experience.)

3. **What do they need from you?** (Clarity about boundaries and limits, explanation of decisions, support to be on hand, space to be heard, invitation to help solve the problem.)

Before you decide on a strategy, be careful about your thinking: if you don't take the time to consider the outcome questions, the consequence or strategy you choose may be counter-productive. Taking time to identify the desired outcomes means you can select a strategy that will deliver them.

More on outcomes

Our experience of working with schools makes us all too aware of the pressures that can affect decisions about outcomes:

- What do you want as outcomes if you are the teacher who is expected to handle the situation?
- What does the school (as an organisation) want? Is it 'cracking down' on this sort of behaviour? Or does it see these things as inevitable stuff that happens and here is a 'teachable moment'?
- What do you want for the other young people who were watching or who 'know'?
- What do you want for the parents of these young people (given that if you don't get it right, they may be on the phone with complaints)?
- What outcomes are even possible in a busy, time-pressured school day?

So let's go back to the Sam and Kyle incident … …

Outcomes for the Sam and Kyle incident

… Let's freeze time just before you intervene with Sam and Kyle and list some possible desirable outcomes:

- Sam to stop the bullying behaviour and to understand how miserable it makes Kyle feel

- Kyle to feel safe as a result of your response and not to be further at risk, including 'payback'

- The relationship between Sam and Kyle to be repaired and their future dealings with each other to be respectful and trouble-free

- Bystanders (friends of Sam and Kyle and witnesses) who supported the bullying behaviour tacitly or explicitly to understand their responsibilities

- The community to trust that the school will respond to bullying behaviour by getting things fixed without making matters worse

- The parents of these young people not to feel the need to contact the school with complaints about how 'the system' dealt with the problem

- The relationships between all parties (including you) to be strengthened by the response *simply because it has been fair*

Fairness – does it matter?

So, once you are clear about desired outcomes, how can you increase the likelihood of achieving them? We think **fairness**, which we've mentioned several times now, is part of the answer.

Any educator or parent knows, often from bitter experience, that when young people experience a response as unfair, they are typically angry and resentful towards the decision-maker and are not reflective about their *own* behaviour.

You cannot be serious!

It is important that the response you choose promotes reflection and reduces resentment – as far as possible! One way to do this is to move away from consistency of consequence (predetermined sanctions) and focus on **fair process**. When young people experience fair process, they will more readily accept the consequences. It produces meaningful compliance and increased cooperation.

Delivering fair process

What do we mean by fair process? Put simply: *it's a process that engages the people who **have** the problem **in** the problem solving*. It meets people's need to be heard and understood and to be part of the decision making. Fair process is underpinned by values such as:

Respect
Participation
Cooperation
Safety
Collaboration
Empowerment
Equality
Inclusion

Fair process can help turn any incident into a 'teachable moment' and hopefully contribute to the development of social and emotional competencies. It can also reinforce expectations, limits, and the school's values.

Fair process is likely to meet the needs of all those involved in the Sam and Kyle story. But why should you bother even to think about the needs of someone like Sam who has caused all the problems in the first place?

Triangle of needs

If people's needs aren't met by the process or strategy you choose, the parties involved will not be satisfied with the 'solution'. This applies not only to students and teachers but to parents, support staff and the broader school community.

When it comes to 'justice', people have three types of interdependent needs which must all be met if those involved in the problem are to be satisfied with the outcome and with how a solution is reached. This can be best achieved by using fair process.

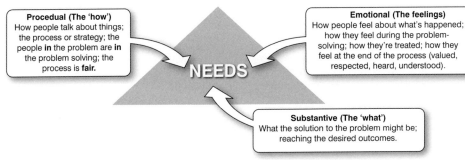

Procedual (The 'how')
How people talk about things; the process or strategy; the people **in** the problem are **in** the problem solving; the process is **fair**.

Emotional (The feelings)
How people feel about what's happened; how they feel during the problem-solving; how they're treated; how they feel at the end of the process (valued, respected, heard, understood).

NEEDS

Substantive (The 'what')
What the solution to the problem might be; reaching the desired outcomes.

Adapted from: Moore, C., (2003). **The Mediation Process**, Jossey-Bass, San Francisco

Substantive needs for Sam and Kyle

Satisfaction

Substantive needs are those that are met in the final decision or plan to solve the problem and to provide satisfaction – the 'what'. Clearly *something* needs to happen.

- You don't want Sam to 'get away' with what he's done
- You don't want Kyle to think we don't care
- You don't want other pupils to think that it's OK to do this stuff
- You don't want to make things worse for any of them (or you!)
- You do want the problem solved efficiently, so we can get about our business quickly

You are more likely to get the substantive outcomes you want if you pay attention to meeting the procedural and emotional needs of the people in the problem. Read on!

Procedural satisfaction for Sam and Kyle

Getting both Sam and Kyle involved in the problem-solving process is important. Just as important as avoiding cries of 'unfair!'.

So you must **maximise engagement**. (Remember, if you are **in** the problem, you get to be involved **in** the problem solving). And the process needs to be experienced by all involved as **fair**. What does this look like in practice?

In the Sam and Kyle scenario, both boys (and possibly others) are involved in the actual process of problem solving, with the teacher acting as a *facilitator* rather than a disciplinarian. They both need a voice – to talk about the incident and have a say in how to make things right.

This is very different from *you* deciding how the matter should be dealt with.

Emotional satisfaction for Sam and Kyle

If Sam and Kyle are not happy with the *process,* it is unlikely that their **emotional needs** will be met. It's worth remembering how we as adults feel if we've been treated unfairly: frustrated, angry, bitter, resentful, etc. To avoid this ensure that:

- People feel safe during the process. This is true for *anyone* involved in the process – parents, young people, staff
- There will be no repercussions after the process for anyone, regardless of their role in the incident
- People are treated with respect and dignity: they are listened to, they have a say, they feel understood, they don't lose face and are not deliberately humiliated

Never underestimate how empowering it is to be listened to and understood, regardless of one's role in the problem. This is fundamental to the concept of fair process.

What about the teacher's needs?

Sometimes it's easy to forget your own needs in this scenario. There's so much pressure on teachers to get through the curriculum, to solve problems quickly, to restore order, to meet everyone else's needs. Apart from needing a break and a cup of coffee, you need to feel that:

- You are competent to be able to confront and respond effectively to all forms of minor wrongdoing in your classroom
- The classroom and its relationships can be restored so that learning is not disturbed
- The students involved don't bear resentment towards you
- Your authority is not undermined
- You will be supported by your managers

How about parents' needs?

Parents have needs too. They need to know that:

- Their son/daughter is safe while at school
- Their child is doing the right thing and staying out of trouble
- Nothing is interfering with their child's learning
- The school has their child's best interests at heart
- If their child is in trouble, that child will be treated fairly

If a school says it *'provides a safe and supportive environment where individual needs are catered for and pupils are taught to be responsible global citizens'*, parents want to see this in action.

We know all too well what happens when parents' needs are not met regarding a harmful incident involving their child. If they feel the process has been unfair, or that their child's voice has not been adequately heard or understood, then teachers get the brunt of their anger and frustration.

When it's sorted, it's over!

Fair process that meets everyone's needs allows everyone to accept that **we all make mistakes**, but then we need to be able to **move on and put the problem behind us**. This is as true for the wrongdoer as it is for the victim. Some might call this forgiveness.

- Once the issue is sorted, it's over
- Past incidents are not dredged up to further punish and stigmatise the wrongdoer
- The emphasis is on separating the deed from the doer

If this can be managed, then the risk of payback is greatly reduced for the victim, or indeed anyone involved, including the teacher.

Putting it all together – measuring success

Looking back at Sam and Kyle, of the four responses on page 14 – **not, for, to** or **with** – only the restorative 'with' response delivers the desired outcomes. It:

- Addresses the needs of those responsible and those affected
- Addresses the needs of the school
- Puts whole school values and beliefs into practice
- Repairs and restores relationships
- Provides that teachable moment for pupils
- Promotes the relationship between teacher and pupil
- Makes you feel OK about missing your coffee break

The need to uphold school values

Even the smallest teacher interventions have an impact on the wider school community. Senior managers, other teachers and the governing body will be concerned about the messages sent to the wider school community about what's right and wrong; how the matter was handled; and how we want young people to think and behave. They will want to know that the school values are being upheld and they need to know that that policies and practices are working to provide a safe school and productive classrooms.

We strongly believe that any response to wrongdoing, no matter how minor or how serious, ought to be a reflection of the school's values and expectations, and of its beliefs about the best way to raise children into responsible, contributing citizens.

But let's make sure that such beliefs are guided by the latest knowledge about brain development and child-rearing, and that subsequent responses are guided by best practice. The next chapter will explain in detail what a simple, low level restorative response looks like.

Restorative Responses

Six stages for Sam and Kyle

If you believe that it's important to do something about what you just witnessed between Sam and Kyle and you choose the restorative option, you will need to consider all those things discussed in the previous section. This means a particular sort of dialogue between you and the pupils.

Let's look at a simple six-stage process for constructing a 'restorative' conversation with Sam and Kyle:

 Engagement – inviting both pupils into the dialogue.

 Reflection – encouraging thoughtfulness and empathy.

 Understanding how people have been affected, ie the harm done.

 Acknowledgement of the harm done and possible apology.

 Agreement – making a plan to fix things.

 Arranging for follow-up – making sure the plan is working.

Engagement

Begin by inviting both boys into the dialogue. Taking Sam and Kyle aside, out of earshot of the other students, say quietly and calmly:

'No one is in trouble, but we need to talk about what just happened.'

How you approach this conversation brings into play what you believe about the importance of doing this work and the importance of keeping everybody's dignity intact (getting the relationships right, promoting respectful classrooms, accommodating the need to 'save face', etc).

It is about problem solving and not about blame. We need to influence brain chemistry so that students communicate and don't duck for cover. This is the beginning of 'teaching them a lesson'.

 **Reflection**

Stage 2 is about encouraging thoughtfulness and empathy. It needs to be handled with care. Don't rush this opportunity for reflection. It's important for Kyle to understand why this has happened to him and for Sam to understand himself and his motivation.

You say:

'Sam, when you tripped Kyle and then pushed him over, what were you thinking?'

This is an invitation delivered respectfully, in a tone of polite but firm enquiry and not with clenched jaws, so that Sam can begin the business of explaining himself. The question needs to include an unambiguous statement of what happened:

'When you tripped Kyle and then pushed him over...'

You give Sam no chance at all of denying what happened. This is on-the-spot problem solving! Make sure you give Sam time to construct an answer – **don't** tell him what he was thinking.

 **Reflection**

If Sam struggles to answer the 'thinking' question, there is a host of alternatives that will deliver a more useful response than *'I don't know'*, *'nothing'*, or a shoulder shrug!

- *'What were you hoping would happen?'*
- *'What was the purpose of doing that?'*
- *'What were you expecting would happen?'*
- *'What did you want when you did that?'*
- *'What was going on in your head when you were doing that?'*
- *'What made you decide to do that?'*
- *'If you did know what you were thinking, what would it be?'*

Be careful that last one doesn't come across as sarcasm!

 NB These 'thinking' questions avoid the use of *'why?'* which we have discovered to be particularly ineffective! It is also vital that, having asked the question, you pause to give the pupil time to collect his/her thoughts. And do remain neutral; don't restate or rephrase what is said – allow the people involved to make their own sense of what they hear.

 **Reflection**

The purpose of these 'thinking' questions is manifold. They will:

- Help Sam reflect on what he has done
- Help all of you, including Sam, to understand his motivation/intention. It's also very important for Kyle to understand *'Why me?'*
- Give you some insight into Sam's maturity, both emotional and moral
- Help you understand whether or not there was any hint of payback for some previous incident involving Kyle
- Help you to understand how Sam makes decisions

They might also give you some feedback on how your classroom management may have inadvertently contributed to the incident.

Remember: ditch the 'why' question – it's not nearly as effective as the 'thinking' question.

 # Reflection

The second stage of the process will also help you establish Sam's capacity for empathy. Remember that one of the outcomes of restorative practice is that children come to understand the harm they can do to others so that they make better choices in the future.

> **You say:**
>
> *'Sam, how do you think Kyle has been affected? What's it been like for him?'*

The purpose of this question is to have Sam begin to think about the impact of his behaviour on Kyle (the victim). It is unlikely that he will be absolutely correct in his assessment of the impact, but it's another reflective question aimed at promoting Sam's level of empathy and compassion.

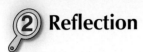 **Reflection**

Often, when something like this happens, more people than just the primary victim are affected. The following question, again reflective, is designed to help Sam think this through.

You say:

'Has what you've done affected anyone else?'; 'Who?'; 'How?'

Here Sam is required to think more broadly. He may 'get it'. He may not. You may have to help by asking:

'What about all the other students who were watching?'
'What about me? How does this affect me?'

 NB In this educative process you must use guiding questions, no lecturing! And always separate the deed from the doer, eg *'Might other people feel unsafe when this sort of thing happens?'*

3 Understanding the harm/impact

Next you invite Kyle to contribute to the conversation.

You turn to Kyle and ask:
'What did you think when Sam first tripped you and then pushed you over?'

And then:
'What was that like for you?'
'What was the worst of it?'

The purpose of these questions, directed to the *victim* is to **establish what harm has been done**. Kyle's answers will help Sam realise that what was possibly a game for him had unhappy consequences for someone else. This part of the process also helps Kyle to realise the hurt for himself and to express it in an appropriate way, reducing the risk of payback later on.

3 Understanding the harm/impact

It might now be useful to ask and answer those same questions about yourself:

> *'Sam, Kyle, do you have any idea of the impact this has on me?'*

It will help Sam and Kyle to understand that teachers are real people too, eg:

> *'It's held me up getting some equipment from the office for the next lesson and now I'll be running late.'*

This is not about making a martyr of yourself, but rather getting both of them to think more broadly.

You may also choose to make some value statement, eg:

> *'It is important that we have fun here at school, but it's not OK to do that at someone else's expense, and it's not right that teasing goes too far and that Kyle should be humiliated. School needs to be a safe place for everyone.'*

The simple questions in stages 2 and 3 will do the job of making Sam accountable without resorting to labelling either boy as victim or wrongdoer or telling them they are bad people because of what they did.

④ Acknowledgement

'Sam, since we have been talking and we have listened to Kyle what have you been thinking about?'

If he has difficulty understanding this question it has various other forms:

'Sam, now we are here talking about what happened, what is going on in your head?'

'Now we are here talking about what happened with Kyle, what have you thought about?'

'What do you think now about what you did? Was it helpful?'

The question asks Sam to reflect on what has happened. It needs to be asked after he has had time to **think** and hopefully **reflect** on his behaviour and its impact on his peers and others. It provides a snapshot of social and emotional growth and of Sam's **thoughtfulness** about others.

④ Acknowledgement

Next, you turn to Sam and say:

'Sam, what could you say to Kyle right now about what happened? What does he need to hear from you?'

Hopefully, this will elicit an apology from Sam to Kyle. If there's no history of bad blood between the boys, the apology should come easily. You may not hear the word 'sorry', but instead something that acknowledges the harm caused. Don't make assumptions about Sam knowing how to formulate a genuine apology. Apologising is an advanced social skill that is both a science and an art form. Sam may never have learnt how to do it!

Ideally, Sam will also say something about making *you* late. If he doesn't, you'll have to make a decision on the spot about whether or not you want to insist on an apology for yourself by asking, *'And what could you say to me so I feel better about this?'*

5 Agreement – making a plan to fix things

The next stage in the process is to work towards fixing things.

You ask Kyle:

'What could Sam do to make things right for you?'

Check his suggestions with Sam:

'Would that be OK? Is that fair?'

Ask both of them:

'Do you have any other suggestions?'

Sam and Kyle are the ones who contribute to *their* agreement. Your role is to facilitate, not judge, or rescue, or impose your own ideas. If you want to offer a suggestion, do it tentatively. You'll also need to offer some reality checks around their ideas, eg *'Is that achievable?'*, *'What would that look like?'*

6. Arranging for follow-up

Ask both boys:

'How should we follow this up? Any suggestions?'

Then say:

'I'll just make a note of what we've agreed.

Shall I check with both of you tomorrow at the end of lunch to see how the agreement is going? Shall we meet here?

Thanks both of you for helping to sort this out.

Have a great day!'

It makes sense to follow up on what was agreed. This will teach both boys that you mean business and at our school 'people stick to their agreements'.

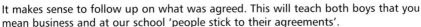

It is the certainty of the follow-up that puts teeth in the process, and gives valuable feedback about the effectiveness of what you've done. Make time for it!

The restorative chat

What you've just read are the bare bones of a restorative process, typically called the **restorative chat**.

- You've handed the problem back to the people who had it (Sam and Kyle)
- You've worked *with* them
- You've used a process that has made Sam accountable first to Kyle and perhaps to you and other students
- You've given Kyle a voice

All that without having to resort to punishment! And, what's more, having **restored** things between the two students, you have, as an added bonus, **strengthened your relationship** with both Sam and Kyle. The restorative process leaves all parties with their sense of self-worth intact, dignity restored, relationships healed and little – if any – resentment towards you. They'll know that you mean business but are prepared to help them. What a bargain!

(You'll find a summary script for this simple and effective 'chat' on page 117.)

Restorative chat and social discipline

If we go back to the Social Discipline Window on page 14 and take the top right hand quadrant, we can add some more detail:

A Restorative Process delivers:
- **Consistency**
- **Responsiveness**
- **Flexibility**
- **Cooperation**
- **Negotiation**
- **Accountability**
- **Responsibility**
- **Collaboration**
- **High expectations**

We have worked *'with'* Sam and Kyle doing what effective teachers do each and every day in their classrooms.

High Control: set limits, discipline

High Support: encourage, guide, nurture

The Restorative Continuum

The punitive continuum

So far we've outlined the restorative response to a low level incident. What happens, though, when the incident is more serious?

We're all familiar with the rising scale of sanctions applied in the traditional punitive model of discipline. What's important in this model is that the level or type of wrongdoing triggers a predetermined consequence.

Category of Behaviour / Wrongdoing

• Talking out of turn	• Vandalism	• Bullying	• Physical assault
• Refusal	• Swearing	• Littering	• Abuse of a teacher
• Lateness/homework	• Truancy	• Theft	• Violence/Harassment

'The more serious the behaviour the tougher the sanction'

• Scolding	• Detention	• Isolation in/out	• Suspension	• Expulsion
• Rebuke	• Loss of privilege	of classroom	• Contract	• Exclusion

Predetermined Consequence / Punishment

Introducing the restorative continuum

The restorative continuum covers a range of restorative processes according to the levels of wrongdoing and harm caused in the wake of an incident. What's important *here* is that the people who are IN the problem are involved IN the problem solving.

Process				
• Restorative Dialogue/Chat	• Small Group Conference	• Large Group Conference	• Classroom Conference	• Community Conference

'The more serious the harm done the more formal will be the response'

• Teacher and student	• Teacher and several students	• Teachers and whole class	• Teachers, parents and students
Participants			

Put simply, the 'community' responsible **for** and affected **by** the behaviour deliberate and decide on consequences aimed at **making things right**. This is in direct contrast to the punitive continuum where the sanctions are predetermined, and the community of people affected has no say in the outcomes.

Managing the big discipline incidents

This begs the question about the seriousness of incidents. Who decides whether an incident is a big deal or not? The member of staff who inherits the problem or the community affected by what has happened?

Who would be closest to the problem and have the best understanding of it?

Restorative justice proposes that the people who know the problem best are those who were directly involved in the incident, ie those who did it and those who had it done to them. If we impose predetermined sanctions, how can these consequences meet the needs of those affected?

This does **not** mean that the school backs away from dealing with a serious incident with a serious response or goes soft on wrongdoing; rather it takes a different approach to problem solving because it views the problem in a different way.

What do we mean by the bigger discipline incidents?

Let's have a quick look at what might influence how disciplinary incidents are viewed by schools. In an **authoritarian-punitive** school, the factors that might influence whether an incident is 'big' (and therefore deserving a serious response) include:

- How many rules have been broken and the number of times they were breached
- The messages that need to be sent to the wider school community about 'this sort of thing'
- The degree to which the authority of teachers has been ignored or threatened
- The wrongdoer's track-record and the family's connection and history with the school
- The disciplinary philosophy of the school/senior managers/directors/governors
- The history and profile of 'this sort of behaviour' across the school (is it the flavour of the month? Is there a crackdown on it?)
- An ingrained philosophy of retribution
- The level of distress/anger/injury of the victims, and their status and position
- Skills and attitudes of staff and managers caught in the middle of the incident
- How the level of blame directed at the school can be deflected

Restorative big deals

In an **authoritative-restorative** school, the influencing factors include:

- The depth and breadth of the harm done (material, relational, emotional)
- The readiness of wrongdoer, victim and their various support groups to participate willingly in a process built not on a philosophy of retribution, but on repair and healing. This depends on the wrongdoer being willing to admit their part in what happened
- What outcomes *all* the parties involved, including the school, might want
- The belief that holding someone accountable does not necessarily involve punishment, but does involve the wrongdoer facing up to those affected and taking responsibility for the impact of their behaviour
- A willingness to take the time to achieve a lasting fix
- A willingness to reflect on how the system may have contributed to the problem (collective responsibility)
- A philosophical belief that the people who are in the problem are the best ones to decide how to fix it (with appropriate process and support)
- A belief that problem solving is about righting the wrongs and repairing the harm
- An awareness of the risks if effective, appropriate action is not taken

Moving from punitive to restorative

To make the move from punitive to restorative, what's needed is a different way of thinking about problems. So rather than the punitive approach of:

'What rules were broken and by whom?'

ask yourself:

'Who's responsible and who has been affected?'

You'll know better how serious an incident is once you have spoken with the main people involved and asked some simple questions to gauge the extent of the harm.

Once you have assessed the extent of the harm, thought about what outcomes you want for the various groups of people affected and considered how best to meet their needs, you can choose the appropriate response from the restorative continuum.

The next two chapters take you further along the continuum from the restorative chat to the Small Group Conference and, finally, to the Community Conference, but first a quick word about shame.

A quick word about shame

We all know the sense of shame that comes when we have done the wrong thing or behaved inappropriately. Some schools make the mistake of thinking they need to shame wrongdoers, making them feel so humiliated that they 'won't do it again'. This is actually counter-productive because *deliberate shaming* invites defensive behaviours that tend to make matters worse.

And it is not always understood that victims also experience shame when what happens to them somehow diminishes them in the eyes of others and themselves. If those involved are part of a process that encourages reflection, acknowledgement and understanding and focuses on making things right, shame can be acknowledged and discharged. This not only makes all parties feel better about themselves, they stay connected to their significant others and their support group. Indeed, these connections are often strengthened.

Processes such as the Community Conference (pages 122-124) that produce these sorts of positive social outcomes, are restorative and reintegrative.

Introducing
Restorative
Practice

 Relationships
and Fair
Process

 Restorative
Responses

 The
Restorative
Continuum

 The Small
Group
Conference ◄

 The Big
Discipline
Issues

 Final Words
of Advice

The Small
Group
Conference

Back to Sam and Kyle

To understand more about the restorative continuum and how it might work for you, let's consider the Sam and Kyle incident, but this time the circumstances in Ms Clark's classroom are more serious.

The incident
As the class are leaving for morning break Sam trips Kyle, who falls to the floor. As he gets up, Sam pushes him and he crashes into Ria, who falls and bangs her head against a desk. Sam then shoves his way past Lexie causing her to drop her graphic calculator, which lands on the floor and appears to be damaged. Ms Clark calls out for Sam to stop and come back, which he does promptly.

Serious trouble for Sam

The issues
Any break for Ms Clark is now certainly disrupted as it is school policy that a first aid officer is called to attend any head-related injury. Lexie, meanwhile, is assessing the damage to her calculator, not knowing what to do. She is trying to make eye contact with Ms Clark to gain her assistance.

The incident is more serious than the previous scenario in that it has affected more people and in different ways, including physical injury and property damage. It requires a more 'serious' response from the teacher and the likely involvement of a senior member of staff.

Ms Clark, feeling very upset and angry, informs all four pupils that she will need to speak with the Head of Year Mr Kent to discuss what will happen next and she will get back to them with a decision before the end of the day. They are then dismissed for the break knowing that they will be required to meet later to work things out. In schools new to this approach, the process will need to be carefully explained.

Applying the restorative continuum

1. Ms Clark discusses the incident with Mr Kent.

2. Both decide that the best way forward is to use a Small Group Conference with those involved. Parents will be notified of the incident and informed about the response. This decision is usual school policy.

3. Mr Kent offers to facilitate the conference the following day after school.

4. Mr Kent meets with all four students to explain the conference process, gain agreement that this is the most appropriate way to resolve things, and to go over stories and the order of events. He advises them to stay calm and not do anything that would escalate the situation.

5. Mr Kent contacts the parents to explain the incident, what role their child played, the process that will be used, the issues that need to be discussed, and confirms that he will contact all families immediately after the conference.

6. Mr Kent meets with Ms Clark to keep her informed and updated.

7. Mr Kent meets with Sam and Kyle the next day to prepare the room and refreshments for the conference.

Setting up the Small Group Conference

The conference will be held in a vacated classroom that can provide a quiet and interruption-free space for 30-60 minutes. The Head of Year will use similar questions to those on page 118, a 'script' that asks a series of questions of each person in a set order dependent on their role in the incident.

The first person to speak will be Sam. This will help him explain to the others what motivated him to behave the way he did and to begin taking responsibility for his actions. This will be followed by the other students and their teacher explaining how the incident has affected them and *together* they can decide about how to put things right between them all.

Mr Kent's role is that of facilitator. He does not speak *for* anyone. He may take an active role in the agreement stage by making some suggestions if the boys are getting stuck for ideas. If the incident is resolved properly, there will be no backlash, no escalating conflict and best of all, the boys will have renewed respect for their teacher and Head of Year because the approach they took was helpful, did not involve punishment, and preserved the dignity of all parties.

Seating plan

Participants sit in a circle without any object (eg table) in between people

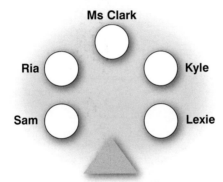

Head of Year as facilitator

Step 1 – Introduction

The facilitator invites the students and their teacher into the room and to take a seat before explaining the rules of engagement.

The facilitator says:

'Thank you for making the time to be here this afternoon. This conference is not about blaming anyone for what they did but a chance for us all to understand what has happened and who has been affected. Your honesty has been helpful in finding out what happened yesterday and this meeting is an opportunity to take responsibility for any part you played and to suggest how you can make things right. It is a chance to tell us how each of you feels about what has happened and what needs to be done to repair any harm that any of you have experienced.

In our planning meetings we discussed how we will show respect for each other today and who will speak first. I need to remind you that your parents have been informed about this meeting and they will receive a copy of any agreement that we reach here today. Let us begin.'

Step 2 – Reflection

Some possible responses:

Sam, can you tell us what was going on when you tripped up and then pushed Kyle?	It started with Kyle not lending me his ruler. I wanted to ask him why he wouldn't and Ms Clark thought I wasn't working. I wanted to do a good job of my graph and I got frustrated so I tripped him up when we were leaving for break. We have been pushing and tripping each other up for a while.
Sam, can you tell us a bit more about that? (the tripping and pushing) How long has it been happening?	Well, I guess about a week now, since some of the Year 11 boys did it to us at the lockers.
Sam, what were you thinking when you rushed out of the classroom knocking Lexie's calculator out of her hands?	I thought I'd be in real trouble when Ria hit her head on the desk so I wanted to get out fast. I just made things worse when Lexie dropped her calculator. I didn't mean to involve Lexie. I was just being stupid I guess.

Step 2 – Reflection

Some possible responses:

Sam, what have you been thinking about since yesterday?	Well, I didn't mean to hurt anyone. I've made a big problem for my class. I shouldn't have got angry with Kyle.
How about the pushing and tripping?	It's pretty stupid. We need to stop, but it's hard when the Y11s do it to us all the time round the lockers.
Sam, can you talk about who has been affected by what you did?	Well, Ria… I didn't mean for Kyle to crash into you. I am worried that Lexie's calculator might be broken. You (Mr Kent) spent a lot of yesterday trying to sort out what happened. My parents think I am mucking around all day at school and I've made things pretty bad for Kyle.
Who else? How about Ria's art group and Ms Clark?	Well, they couldn't do their group project in art because Ria was in the medical room. Ms Clark is a great teacher… she didn't deserve what I did yesterday.
Kyle, can you think of anyone else?	I guess the class…I disrupted people from working when I was teasing Sam.

Step 3 – Understanding the harm done

Some possible responses:

Kyle, what did you think when Sam tripped and pushed you?	I didn't know if he was playing a game or if he was really upset with me when he barged out of the room. I guessed he was upset.
How did you feel about what happened?	I felt pretty embarrassed falling down in front of the class. I feel bad for Ria and Lexie. Maybe it was my fault. If I had lent him my ruler all this stuff might not have happened.
Ria, what did you think when you were knocked over by Kyle?	I'm sick of them mucking around. I'll probably not get into the drama production because I had a big headache from hitting my head yesterday.
What has been the worst thing for you about this?	Like I said, I want to get into the drama production and my audition was yesterday. I am worried that this might happen to me again…they never stop playing stupid games like this.

Step 3 – Understanding the harm done

Some possible responses:

Lexie, what did you think when Sam barged past you causing you to drop your calculator?

Like Ria, all this mucking around they do has caused lots of problems. I've checked my calculator and it works OK but the cover is broken. I have to deal with Mr Jones who leases the calculators to us and he said they cost a fortune and we have to pay for any damage.

So what is the main thing that bothers you about all this?

Well the trouble with my parents. They said if I could show some responsibility with my calculator they might get me the latest mobile phone. I thought I would have no chance until Mr Kent called and explained to my parents what happened.

Step 3 – Understanding the harm done

Some possible responses:

Ms Clark, what did you first think when this happened?	I was really shocked when Ria was pushed into the desk. It was unbelievable that something so trivial over a ruler could end up with Ria in the medical room and Lexie's calculator being broken.
What has been the worst thing for you about this?	The worst… I am worried that Mr Jones won't look upon me as a good teacher if his calculators are being damaged in my class. Sam and Kyle have so much potential… such good students until they sit together in class.
Ms Clark, what are the main issues for you about this incident?	I'm very upset and the issue for me is that I really don't know what to do about this. Sometimes you can both be very thoughtful of others and then this nonsense happens. I wonder if all this mucking around happens in other classes, or just in mine?

Step 4 – Acknowledgement and apology

Some possible responses:

Sam, is there anything you want to say at the moment... what have you learnt from listening to people today?

I don't know about the drama audition... I'm sorry Ria. Maybe if I talk to the Head of Drama he might give you another try? And the calculator, now I know why the broken cover is a big deal... I will swap my calculator for Lexie's if that will work. I didn't mean to make things bad for you at home, Lexie. Maybe I can write your parents a note explaining that it wasn't your fault?

Is there anybody else who might need to hear something from you?

Well, Ms Clark, you are a really good teacher and maybe we need to stop mucking around in your class – and it's all classes, Miss. We actually mess around less in your class because we think you are really cool. I don't know what I can do about Mr Jones.

Step 4 – Acknowledgement and apology

Some possible responses:

How about Kyle?	Oh, sorry for making you look stupid in class yesterday.
Kyle says...	That's OK. Sorry for teasing you… and Ria I hope your headache gets better and you get into the drama show. I think we need to stop sitting next to each other. We just can't stop messing about when we are together in every class.
Lexie says...	I guess I didn't help when I told you not to give Sam your ruler and then I was laughing when he was getting upset.

Step 5 – Agreement. Making a plan and arranging follow up

Some possible responses:

Ria, what would you like to see happen as a result of this conference?	I appreciate Sam saying that he will see the HOD but there is a second audition if I don't get in, so things might be OK. I could give Sam one of my spare rulers so this doesn't happen again? I know it wasn't Kyle's fault for pushing me into the desk.
Lexie, what needs to happen to make things right for you?	Well, it's not just the ruler thing. It's all the tripping up stuff. Yesterday it got out of control. I really want it to stop.
How about your calculator?	I'm not sure how it will work if we just swap. They all have serial numbers on them. Mr Kent explained to my parents that it wasn't my fault the calculator was broken. And they were impressed that I am giving up my time to be here tonight so that got me some points.
Sam says...	This is my problem so I will go and ask Mr Jones if he can swap the serial numbers and I will explain that I will pay for the damage to the broken one... OK.

Step 5 – Agreement. Making a plan and arranging follow up

Some possible responses:

Ms Clark, what do you want as an outcome from today?	It is very satisfying to hear Sam trying to work out a calculator exchange. If Sam and Kyle are serious about stopping the messing about they will need to sit away from each other without me asking them every lesson. I want Ria to feel safe in my classroom but I also think we need to do something about the Y11s and what's going on around the lockers.
Mr Kent says...	I will take the problem at the lockers to our next Head of Year meeting and see what we can do to address the behaviour. What else do we need to include in our agreement? Does sitting separately include every class Sam...Kyle?
Sam and Kyle both say...	Yes.
Mr Kent says...	Do we need to write down what we are agreeing on here today? So far we have agreed to do the following...

Wrapping up the conference

The conference continues to develop a solid plan about who will do what so that everybody can move forward and issues are resolved. This is called 'the conference agreement'. The conference ends when everyone has been invited to contribute to the agreement and is clear about what they have been asked to do. In the Sam and Kyle incident the agreement might include the following:

- Sam apologised to all involved for his behaviour
- Kyle apologised to Sam for teasing him and both promised to stop the tripping and pushing
- Sam and Lexie will ask Mr Jones if they can arrange a swap of calculators
- Sam will arrange with Mr Jones to pay for the damage to the calculator
- Sam and Kyle will not sit together in Ms Clark's class or any other class
- Mr Kent will follow up on the behaviour of the Y11s at the lockers
- The four students will meet with Mr Kent each week for an appropriate length of time to check on progress and whether the plan is holding
- Ms Clark and the four students will report back to the class about the plan
- Mr Kent will send a copy of this agreement to each family and each student

Closing the conference

Mr Kent formally thanks everybody for their participation and then invites everyone to share some refreshments together if time permits. It's really worth considering the importance of this symbolic ritual.

'Breaking bread' or sharing refreshments at the end of a Small Group Conference is part of the ritual of reintegration and reconnection for people whose relationships have been damaged. To have Lexie, Ria, Kyle, Sam, Ms Clark and Mr Kent together, talking informally with each other, and at the same time offering each other food and drink is helpful in bringing closure to a harmful incident. The healing and forgiveness that is often visible at these moments gives real meaning to the term 'supportive school community'.

The Big Discipline Issues

Serious stuff

The 'No Blame Classroom Conference' (see pages 119-121) and the formal Community Conference are natural extensions of the Small Group Conference. Imagine this scenario:

For several weeks now the classroom teacher/s have been complaining of disruptive behaviour, eg students not on task, lots of chatter, low level teasing and pranks, lack of respect for the classroom. The teacher/s are feeling like they spend the whole day reprimanding students.

Usually facilitated by someone in the school with appropriate training, the 'No Blame Classroom Conference' is the first experience of restorative justice for many students. It engages the whole class in a problem-solving process that encourages reflection, mutual understanding, and shared ownership of the problems that people are experiencing. The class, together with their teacher/s, plan a way forward aiming for a more positive learning environment.

Take care! Using restorative processes to quell disruptive classrooms will do more harm if the classroom environment remains authoritarian/punitive. All parties, including teachers, must be willing to examine their behaviour!

The Community Conference

As the behaviour/incidents become more serious, resulting in greater harm, the parents of those involved need to be brought in to provide support and assist the 'community' in deciding what consequences will provide the best learning experiences and repair the harm. This very formal response is called the Community Conference.

A word of caution!

It is at this point that we must caution you about attempting to facilitate a Community Conference without the appropriate professional training. The more formal the approach, the more rigorous the facilitation of the process needs to be. The facilitator really needs to know what they are doing, especially when parents and teachers attend. Excellent training is available (see page 125).

What is a Community Conference?

A **Community Conference** is a face-to-face meeting of the community of people affected by an incident which causes serious harm within the school or community. The conference provides a forum in which wrongdoers, victims and their respective supporters seek ways to identify, repair and prevent future harm in the wake of a serious incident.

Wrongdoers are given an opportunity to explain themselves and to understand the impact of their behaviour on other people, themselves and their school community. They are also invited to make things right by acknowledging the harm they have caused by way of apology or material reparation. **Victims** have the opportunity to explain how they have been affected and to become involved in negotiating how to repair the harm.

A Community Conference will not go ahead if the wrongdoer/s do not admit their involvement or if people do not feel safe as participants in the process, despite a range of support measures being offered. Some reluctance to participate is normal, especially for people experiencing a Community Conference for the first time, but refusal is rare.

Who attends a Community Conference?

- An experienced and trained conference **facilitator**

- The **wrongdoer/s** directly responsible for the incident

- The **victim/s** directly affected by the incident

- The **bystanders/supporters/witnesses** who were there when it happened and were affected, or maybe escalated the issue

- **Other parties affected** by the incident who, owing to their role or position, have to manage the fallout, eg teachers, police officers, etc

- **Supporters for the victims and wrongdoers**, ie people who can provide a sense of safety for the victims and also assist in the exploration of the harm caused. They can also be a resource for reaching agreement and deciding on what needs to be done to repair the harm

Time required

There are two separate time elements: **preparation** and **facilitation**.

Preparation time will depend on the circumstances and complexity of the incident, the number of people involved and how willing they are to participate.

Facilitating the conference will take on average one and a half to two hours. Conferences are usually held within one to five days of the incident occurring.

Sometimes the process is used as the 'ceremony of reintegration' to terminate a fixed term exclusion (suspension), before the pupil is back in class.

Outcomes

The most tangible **outcome** is a written agreement, usually signed by all parties present. The terms of the agreement may include anything from an apology and assurances that the behaviour will stop to:

- Community service work in school or elsewhere (if it makes sense)
- Repayment of money or property if appropriate
- Repair of any damage to property
- Agreement of student or family to access appropriate support, eg counselling

The outcomes are limited only by the group's imagination and its ability to ensure compliance with the terms of the agreement.

Remember though, the process is designed to meet the procedural, emotional and substantive needs of all participants (see page 32). It is NOT designed to agree on a series of punishments, which would defeat the philosophy of repair!

What happens in a conference?

Let's use a more serious scenario involving Sam and Kyle to illustrate the Community Conference. Imagine the following:

As the class is being dismissed for morning break Sam trips Kyle who stumbles to the floor. As he gets up, Sam then pushes him causing him to crash into Ria, who falls against a desk striking her head. Seeing this, Sam panics and in his attempt to escape the trouble, he shoves his way past several students who are leaving the classroom. Lexie's materials, including an expensive calculator, hit the floor with batteries spilling out and the cover flying off. As Sam takes off down the corridor Ms Clark, the teacher, calls out for him to stop but he refuses and shouts, 'No #+*^# way!'.

During break time, Lexie and several of her 'friends' confront Sam about the damage to the calculator. Things get out of hand with some pushing and shoving and loud words. Sam chooses to leave the school grounds. It's all he can think of doing for his own safety after the 'gang' confrontation.

Sam and Kyle continued

After restoring order to the classroom, Ms Clark approaches Mr Kent the Head of Year (HOY) to explain what has happened. It turns out Sam has absconded. Mr Jones, on break duty, saw Sam leaving the premises. Sam ignored his instructions to stop. Mr Jones sent a note to the HOY with the details.

In the wake of this incident we have a head injury, broken calculator, verbal abuse of Ms Clark, 'gang' confrontation and truancy from school. Imagine you are that HOY. You have many issues and a range of needs and possible outcomes to consider before deciding how to respond:

- Teachers want to know what you will do to support Ms Clark and put a stop to this unacceptable behaviour
- When and how will you talk to Sam, Kyle, Ria and Lexie?
- How could you include Ms Clark and Mr Jones in a constructive conversation?

The restorative continuum dictates that this incident be met with a formal response. How might a Community Conference deliver the goods? Let's start by considering the key players. What's going on in their heads?

What's really going on?

Sam

You feel angry because Ms Clark didn't understand what was going on. You were asking Kyle why he wouldn't lend you his ruler so you could do a neat graph. The teacher scolded you, thinking you were chatting and not doing your work. As you left the class you tripped and then pushed Kyle for some payback, partly because he was doing the same to you this morning before school. You didn't mean for Kyle to crash into Ria; you were only mucking around.

To avoid getting into more trouble you decided to get out quickly. That's when Lexie's calculator hit the floor and broke apart. It wasn't deliberate. You can't remember what you yelled at Ms Clark; you just needed to escape.

In the playground you had that anxious feeling in your stomach. Then you were confronted by Lexie and the broken calculator gang. Fearing the worst, you left school and spent the rest of the day in the alley behind the local shops, too frightened to go back to school or to go home. When you did get home you pretended that it was just a normal school day. You know that today's trouble was mostly your doing but you don't know how to begin unwinding the mess.

Kyle's thinking

Kyle

You're at a loss to know what to feel. You know that Sam is in hot water and are very glad that it's not you. But in a niggling sort of way you feel that you might have started some of this trouble by teasing Sam over the ruler.

If it comes out that you and Sam have been tripping and pushing each other as a 'joke' you know your mother will be very upset as you lied to her about how your school trousers got ripped. You were torn between calling Sam on your mobile phone at break time or keeping quiet.

Just before you set off home you were called to Mr Kent's office. You are really worried now!

And the victims

Ria
You were simply minding your own business when you were knocked over by Kyle. This is not the first time that their pushing and shoving has affected you. You try to steer clear of them, worrying what might happen next. Out of embarrassment you told Ms Clark that you were OK but that lump on your forehead is now much bigger. You are glad the first aid officer has arrived as you really don't feel that well. There is the dreadful feeling of things getting worse, especially if Sam and Kyle get into more trouble because of your injury.

Lexie
You knew you would have to report your broken calculator to Mr Jones as it's on loan and any damage must be paid for. Unfortunately, at break your friends convinced you to confront Sam about swapping calculators and for him to deal with the damage, not you. You felt you had to or you'd have lost face with your friends. You didn't really know what to say to Sam and it all got out of hand when the gang circled Sam and started to jostle him. Sam threw a few punches in self-defence before running away. Luckily the gang didn't pursue him. You heard Sam's name over the loud speaker and felt panic – Mr Jones would surely find out about the calculator. Somehow you are feeling this is your fault.

Some 'significant others'

Sam's mother

It is 6:00pm and you have just been telephoned by
Mr Kent about Sam's behaviour. The school has been
attempting to contact you all day and even issued a
missing persons report with the police to cover their duty
of care. The news got worse as you heard that your child used offensive language and
this is maybe why he took off. Mr Kent explained that for Sam's own safety and that
of the staff there is an indefinite suspension in place until you can make it to the
school for a meeting. Tonight's plans for visiting a local restaurant for a family dinner
have taken a sudden turn for the worse.

Kyle's mother

You are not certain what all the fuss is about but you are keen
to understand how your son might be involved in the
damage to the calculator and the physical bullying. You are
satisfied with how the school has been dealing with the
problem so far. Mr Kent has suggested that a Community
Conference might be the best way to resolve things.

Some 'significant others'

Ria's mother and father

You received a phone call from the school office about
Ria being injured in class. The school said that she is OK
and it is school policy that any head-related injury
students are removed from class and placed under observation in the medical room.
You are relieved that she is OK but concerned when you remember a recent comment
from another parent about some of the pranks going on in that class. You make the
connection between your child's head injury and some bullying behaviour that she
might be experiencing. You feel it is time to contact the HOY with your concerns.

Lexie's father

Not being wealthy enough to buy a complex calculator, you have paid a significant
sum as security to allow Lexie to lease one. Mr Kent telephoned you to fill you
in on the incident and to say Lexie was not to blame for the damage. The
HOY also conveyed to you a worrying perception that Lexie's friends tried to
intimidate Sam and this sort of gang behaviour in response to property
damage is very serious. You don't see eye to eye with the HOY on some of
the issues and you ask about the level of supervision of the class and why
some students can't be responsible around such expensive equipment.

The staff who have been affected

Ms Clark
Things today were pretty awful. Dealing with Sam and Kyle is never easy, as they are good friends but rarely work well when together. Time after time you separate them but when you turn your back they have drifted together again. You scolded Sam today for not working as you caught him trying to talk to Kyle several times. You just can't understand why he would try to hurt his friend and then use that foul language towards you. You feel that you have failed to build a good relationship with both pupils and after hearing that Sam had absconded you believe you should have handled this differently.

Mr Jones (teacher on duty)
To be totally ignored by Sam who just walked out of the school gates has left you stunned. You coach Sam in football and felt that your relationship might have meant he would respond to you. Now you feel that perhaps the school and its teachers are losing control of students. You wanted to report Sam's behaviour immediately but you couldn't leave your playground area and then you had a class sitting an important assessment straight after your duty. It is not the first time you've felt isolated when on duty.

More people involved in the incident

Mr Kent (Head of Year)
As HOY you feel frustrated about what seems to be a complete lack of
respect by students for each other and for their teachers. To hear that a
vigilante group confronted Sam over some damage to a calculator is a
great worry. You're concerned that this whole incident is a direct challenge
to the school's authority. You know both of these pupils to be of good
character and always friendly but you're not surprised that they could get
involved in this sort of nonsense. The safety of teachers is a prime concern and the use
of inappropriate language by pupils has been one of your pet projects this term.

Headteacher
This incident has brought to light a lack of communication around the
school, especially serious when an incident like this occurs. The fact that a
duty teacher couldn't immediately report Sam's defiant truancy is
worrying. There was no timetable or class list in the office for the HOY to
find which class Sam should have been in. The HOY reported that he
wasn't able to contact Sam's parents to let them know of Sam's truancy.
The only alternative was to call the police and make a missing persons report.
This was a waste of police resources and a poor reflection on the school's image.

Preparations for the conference

If the best process to try to resolve these issues is a conference, then it is crucial that the facilitator interviews all people involved before deciding the final participant list. These interviews are critical for two purposes:

- To gain a clear understanding of who was involved in the series of incidents and how, and to determine their role in the conference (victim, wrongdoer, supporter, area of responsibility)

- To inform each participant of the conference process, including when they will be asked to speak and the questions they will be asked to respond to

The facilitator will also prepare and send letters informing families of dates and times and other conference information; prepare the conference documents; arrange a suitable room; liaise with the school administration; discuss transportation and childcare needs; organise refreshments. The task of conference facilitator is complex and not for the faint-hearted or unskilled!

The start of Sam and Kyle's conference

It is 5:30 pm and as participants arrive at school they are greeted by the Head.
The conference facilitator ushers them into the classroom where chairs are set out in a
circle. When everybody is present the facilitator formally welcomes everybody,
introducing people by name and their reason for being present. The 'rules of
engagement' are explained setting the formal tone for the conference.

Sam is invited to speak first, followed by Kyle then Ria and Lexie. They tell their stories
explaining why all this happened. Participants also hear about how events have
affected people. Who speaks when is clearly defined: wrongdoers first, then victims
and their supporters, and finally the wrongdoers' supporters.

Ria's family speak about her head injury and their anxiety is apparent as they tell how
a nephew sustained lasting eye damage from similar sorts of fooling around at school.
Last to speak, Sam and Kyle's parents are visibly upset and disappointed. They say they
do not condone this sort of behaviour and expect more from their sons. They also talk
about the impact on the families at home.

The mid-point of the conference

After hearing everybody's story, the facilitator asks Sam, then Kyle and Lexie, if they wish to say anything to the people present. Apologies flow to people who need to hear them. Sam tells Kyle that he shouldn't feel bad; it's all been Sam's fault, not Kyle's. Kyle's mother chips in to thank Sam, but comments that her son made choices as well. Sam tells Ms Clark that she didn't deserve to have this happen in her class as she is a great teacher. Kyle nods in agreement.

Sam apologises for his offensive outburst and explains that he just panicked and didn't intend to cause such upset. Lexie apologises to Sam for not being stronger with her friends. Mr Jones, without prompting, apologises to Sam for 'going off' at him when he walked out of the school gates. If he had known more he would have tried to help in other ways.

The facilitator asks people for their ideas about how to right the wrongs. The parents acknowledge how frustrating Sam and Kyle's behaviour must have been and thank Ms Clark for her patience. The Head affirms the great job Ms Clark is doing as a teacher. Mr Jones offers suggestions for sorting out the matter of the calculator.

Making the conference agreement

The facilitator now assists the group to formulate an agreement that includes plans to **make good any damage**, to **prevent further problems** and to **support** those people in need of it. As people make contributions/suggestions the facilitator checks with the group to gauge whether the requests are fair and realistic. Time is taken to craft a plan that everybody feels is **fair**, will **fix things** and will as much as possible **prevent further harm**. The agreement includes:

- Sam and Kyle have apologised for their behaviour and promised that it will stop

- Sam and Kyle will be allowed to sit together after meeting with Mr Kent who will help them develop a 'Code of Cooperation' aimed at preventing their disruptive behaviour

- Mr Jones will replace Lexie's calculator immediately and Sam will pay for the damage in weekly instalments from his pocket money

Making the conference agreement

- The Head will work with Mr Kent to ensure that duty teachers have radios to communicate with and that class lists and timetables are kept in the office

- Sam has offered to write a letter of apology to the local police for wasting their time. Instead Ms Clark suggested that the class invite the police to give a talk about missing persons as part of their next unit of work. Sam would be responsible for drafting the letter

- Sam and Kyle will write an article in the student newsletter about knowing when having fun is OK and when it is causing harm to other people. They will say that it needs to stop. Ria and Lexie have offered to help with the editing

- It was agreed that the outcomes of the conference would be reported to the class in a classroom conference, and that any other issues that have been affecting learning and relationships would be dealt with there

- Sam's suspension period is formally over

Closing the conference

The facilitator reads out the agreement reached for a final time and then invites people to make any final comments. Some of the parents thank the school for managing this incident in such a constructive manner and thank the teachers for giving up their valuable time.

People are thanked for their participation and invited to 'mingle' around the refreshment table while the agreement is prepared for signing and distribution. This most important stage of 'breaking bread' gives people the chance to reconnect and talk informally. Sam offers a drink to Ria; Kyle takes round a plate of biscuits to Ms Clark and Mr Jones. The Head offers Lexie's father some possible work contacts. Ria's parents head over to Ms Clark to apologise for not contacting her sooner about the bullying rumours they'd heard.

It is now 7:45pm. The facilitator is encouraging people to leave, but they seem to want to stay and keep talking!

Final Words of Advice

Get the basics right

We'd like to conclude this Pocketbook with some advice around the RP basics that we've learnt over the years. We believe that these handy hints will serve you well, whatever your philosophical approach to the management of young people.

Getting it right in the first place is vital. It is worthwhile spending time early in the term or year to begin the process of developing **strong connections**. These strong connections will give you something to work with when inevitable mistakes are made.

It is important to pay attention to the signs that things may not be right, and use restorative processes as a way to **explore the issues** and engage in **healthy problem solving**.

And when things go wrong take the time to **reconnect**!

If you do have to manage the moment of crisis by removing the pupil from your room (or the playground), have a restorative conversation with them before they come back into your class or the playground. This conversation will go a long way to reconnecting you with them and reconnecting them with the others involved.

Spend time on the relationship

The restorative philosophy has reminded both of us, in spite of all our years in classrooms with young people, that we cannot underestimate the importance of the quality of our relationships *with* learners and the quality of the relationships that exist *between* learners.

If the relationship is not right, then the pupil will not engage in learning, and you will find your goodwill and the goodwill of your students eroding.

Be deliberate in your relationship building. Don't leave it to chance. Always remember that young people will respond positively when they think they are liked and respected. Of course, sometimes you will need to work on the issue of respect. It must be unconditional and mutual.

Parents and young brains

We all know that if a positive relationship exists between teacher and parent/caregiver, then it is more likely that engagement in learning will be improved. Most families have a lot riding on their child's time in your classroom. **Think partnership and begin building trust early** with all stakeholders!

Realise that **young brains are a work in progress** and that changing behaviour, or a pattern of behaviour, takes time. It amounts to turning one habit into another which means that the thinking that drives the behaviour has to change too.

Relying on punishment to change thinking and behaviour is unwise. We have to teach young people **how to think** about things. This won't happen by itself. You have to ask the right questions.

Read about brain development. Find out more about the brains of adolescents and what mistakes they make simply because the brain hasn't finished growing – and won't until the mid-to-late-20s. There is still so much you can do, despite difficult family backgrounds or unhelpful circumstances. Sometimes you are their only hope.

Let's say it again: outcomes before strategy

When it comes to disciplinary matters, ask yourself what outcomes you are trying to achieve.

On pages 26-29 we explored the difference between outcomes and strategies. Keep this difference in mind before you default to practices that may well be bad habits. The rule is always to start with the end in mind, even with the most minor infringements. That, combined with some sound understanding and knowledge about what's effective and what's not, should help you make a good decision.

Keep these reflective questions in mind and it's hard to go wrong:

- What do we want them to understand about the situation?
- What changes do we need to see in their behaviour?
- Will a punishment teach them to be more thoughtful/reflective?
- What do we want for the others involved? For ourselves?

First seek to understand

Once you have decided on outcomes (for those who did it, those who had it done to them, and yourself), engage the wrongdoer in a respectful dialogue. Invite them to explain what happened. **Be quiet. Listen!** We tend to talk *at* young people far too much. We tell them they are wrong and bad. We raise our voices. We judge them. We make incorrect assumptions. We give them unhelpful advice, *'you ought'*, *'you should'*, *'you must'*. Relationship and respect become one-way transactions.

Having a **mutually respectful relationship** means taking the time to find out what was happening in the moments beforehand, trying to **see the world from their perspective** before sharing your own, and bringing to light the intention of the behaviour in the first place. Use the restorative dialogue (page 117) when you have this conversation. Ask *'What were you thinking?'* instead of *'Why?'*.

For reflection to become a regular feature of a person's thinking, the skill has to be embedded. This will only happen if you take the trouble to do it over and over. Be repetitive. **Don't give up too soon**. Harness the effect of peer pressure and the need to 'belong' by finding ways for other pupils to give that person feedback on the impact of their behaviour.

Focus on the harm done

When working with pupils concentrate on the harm done rather than the rule broken.

Are they able, with your help, to reflect on the impact of their behaviour on others? When the authoritarian approach to discipline was the norm, teachers simply sought compliance. The only issue was about who was in control.

In this modern era, we have come to understand that compliance for its own sake is not enough. If you want to achieve more than that, the job is to help young people understand more about their behaviour, and its impact on others.

While the rules are still important, having the pupil think about the harm they have done to others and how they can go about 'fixing the broken rule' is the focus. Continue with the restorative dialogue and ask: *'Who do you think has been affected?'; 'In what way?'* or a more specific customised version of this: *'What do you think it has been like for your classmates when you... ...'*

Include those harmed in 'fair' problem solving

Remember **the concept of fairness**. How do we alter our processes so that the people who are in the problem get involved in the problem solving and in that way experience our practice as fair?

If it is at all possible, always aim to include in the dialogue those who have been harmed. It is far more effective when you hear directly from the other party how they have been affected. Ask the people affected, in front of the wrongdoer:

- *'What did you think when this happened?'*
- *'How has this been for you? What's changed?'*
- *'What's been the worst of it?'*

Sometimes it is important to step back from the role of disciplinarian and become the facilitator of a conversation between those who have the problem. You need to feel comfortable with the idea that you don't always have to have the solution, but you do have to provide fair process.

Work on making things right rather than punishment

The restorative philosophy demands that wrongs are righted. In a practical sense, this means that you must ask the question first of the wrongdoer: *'What do you need to do to fix things?'* and then of those wronged: *'What needs to happen to make this right for you?'*

Your job as facilitator is to negotiate sensible plans and build the solution. If any of the parties involved seek to have the wrongdoer punished (eg a detention, fixed term exclusion), ask them first: *'What do you hope that will achieve?'* and then, *'Can you achieve that without resorting to punishment?'*

The purpose of punishment is usually to teach the wrongdoer a lesson, so that they don't do that thing again. The principle is one of suffering – or inconvenience, at least. The risk is that you alienate the pupil, making them resentful and angry with you or with those making the demands. Applying punishment without sufficient thought can make the wrongdoer more *self*-centred and fearful, instead of *other*-centred and respectful.

Model, model, model

Young people are the first to notice if we don't walk the talk, so be prepared to be what you want *them* to be. In our workshops, we ask teachers to define the sorts of skills, character and values they hope to instil in young people in their time at school. The following usually appear in the list:

- Responsibility for the impact of their behaviour on others
- Accountability
- Thoughtfulness/reflection
- Kindness and compassion
- Honesty and trustworthiness
- Reliability
- Integrity
- Respectful and caring behaviour

This means that as teachers *we must be these things ourselves*. The way we manage the relationships in the classroom and beyond must demonstrate the very things we expect. Otherwise, why would anyone pay attention to our exhortations?

Remember who owns the relationship

Traditionally, as a profession, we have relied too heavily on the authority of others to enforce the rules; for instance, expecting someone else to supervise the detentions we have issued, or sending pupils to someone else for punishment. The Deputy or Head of Year has a chat with the pupil and we expect that to do the trick. We get angry when they don't punish the child the way we wanted. This simply does not make sense. The problem *is not being solved where it exists*. We should ask ourselves: 'Who owns the problem?' and 'Who owns the relationship?'

In restorative schools, those in higher authority see their roles differently. They are there to help you sort the problem, not to do it for you. If you must issue a detention, then you supervise it. Don't expect someone else to. You take responsibility for the problem and then ask for help when your strategies and skills are exhausted.

It will be the quality of your relationship with that pupil and that class that will count when things go wrong.

Students and classes have to value the relationship with you for your disapproval of their behaviour to work.

Three golden rules

Remember three golden rules to guide your restorative practice:

Reflect

Repair

Reconnect

In the end, it's the relationships that matter.

The next few pages offer four restorative 'scripts' for use in conferences across the restorative continuum.

1. Restorative Chat script

Individual conference between teacher and student
We need to talk about......

What were you thinking about when you ... ...?
What have you thought about since?
Who has been affected by what you did? In what ways?
How can you fix things?

Some helpful prompts for each question
What did you want to have happen when you did that?
Is what you did helpful?
How do those people feel about what you did?
What can you do or say to make things right?

2. Small Group Conference script

Teacher and several students (wrongdoers and victims)

To the wrongdoer/s – What were you thinking about when you …? What have you thought about since? Who has been affected by what you did? In what ways?

To the victim/s – What did you first think when this happened to you? How do you feel about things now? What has been the worst thing for you?

To the wrongdoer/s – What can you say or do to make things better?

To the victim/s – What would you like to see happen about this? What things need to be said or done to make things right?

To both parties – Does anything else need to happen to repair the harm? Would an agreement help? Is what we have decided on fair? Will it work? Do you need any help from me? Can we move on and put this behind us?

3. 'No Blame Classroom Conference' script

Introduction to class – Thank you for agreeing to participate in a 'No Blame Classroom Conference' which will happen shortly/tomorrow. Before we have our conference we need to understand what harm has been done to people in our class. I would like everybody to take five minutes and write down on the paper provided these things: what has been done to you – the verbal or physical harassment, the name calling or putdowns, etc. Then write down what has been done to others in this class – the words or actions that have been used to hurt people; what you've seen and heard happen. We need to hear about the nastiness, the pushing, the fighting, the teasing, the rumours and the threats (insert whatever is appropriate).

Introduction to conference – Thank you for participating in this conference. This No Blame Classroom Conference will take about one hour. This conference has been called because (insert appropriate statement, eg:

- Your teachers feel they can no longer teach the class and many students in the class are being harmed by what has been happening
- People are not being responsible for their behaviour and other people's right to learn and feel safe is not being respected.)

We want to try to understand who has been affected by the behaviour and in what ways. Everybody will be given a chance to talk about what needs to happen to make things better. People in this class who have been harmed by the behaviour will be given the chance to talk about how they have been affected. This is a 'no blame' conference. No one will get into trouble or be punished for what they say.

3. 'No Blame Classroom Conference' script

Conference rules – *We need to follow some rules so that everybody can be heard and can make a contribution. What is said here today stays in this room. One person speaks at a time; to speak you must be holding our talking stick. You may pass if you wish. You may leave the conference any time you wish but you need to know that the school will manage your behaviour differently if you choose to leave.*

To all participants – *I will now read out some of the statements that you have all made. No names will be mentioned.* **Then:** *I will now roll up all the statements to make our talking stick. What should we call this stick?*

To all teachers present – *Please tell us how you feel about what has been happening in this class. What are the main issues for you?*

To the class – *We will now move round the circle and ask how people feel about what has been done to them and others in this class. Please do not mention any names.*

After the circle has been completed once – *Raise your hand if the talking stick should go round the circle again? (If so, allow this to happen)* **Then:** *Raise your hand if you feel that the behaviour of people in our class and these problems need to stop?*

To the class – *We now want to explore who else has been affected by the behaviour of the class. Who else? Think of the people not here today. Can anybody tell us how ....has been affected? Raise your hand if you are surprised that so many people are affected?*

3. 'No Blame Classroom Conference' script

To the class and teachers – Now it is time for some courage and honesty. It is time to take responsibility for what you have done or said. Remember that no one will be punished. Tell us what you need to do to fix things. You do not need to mention people's names but you might want to say, 'I have put people down by name calling and to those people I apologise', or you may want to say, 'I have pushed and punched Peter and Sam at the lockers and I apologise. I will not do this again'.

After the talking stick has circled once
What else needs to be done to make things better?
Do you accept the apologies that have been given?
What else would you like to see happen?

Involving the bystanders
What things could people do next time......what could they say?
How can the class take some responsibility for what has happened?

Making the agreement – What should our agreement say... ...what things would be helpful? What should our class do if this happens again?

Closing – Is there anything that anybody wants to say before we finish? Thank you for helping us with the conference today. What needs to happen to this talking stick? Where should all the harm and hurt contained in this stick go? Does anybody have any suggestions? Please help us to tidy up the classroom before we leave.

4. Community Conference script

Warning! Attempting to facilitate a Community Conference without appropriate training (see page 125) is as good as professional negligence. There is far too much at risk. Be guided by one of the principles of restorative justice: 'Do no harm'.

1. Introduction

Welcome. As you know, my name is (insert name) and I will be coordinating this conference. Before the conference begins, I would like to introduce everybody briefly and indicate their reasons for being here. (The introductions are usually performed in order around the circle.) At this stage, I would like to thank you all for making the effort to attend. This is a difficult matter, and your participation here will help us deal with it. The conference will focus on the incident (.........) which happened (.........), involving (wrongdoer's and victim's names). It's important to understand that we will focus on what (wrongdoer's name) did and how his/her behaviour has affected others. We are not here to decide whether (wrongdoer's name) is a good or bad person. We want to explore how people have been affected, and see whether we can begin to repair the harm that has been done.

To the wrongdoer(s)

........., you have admitted your involvement in the incident. If at any stage during the conference you no longer wish to participate, you are free to leave – but if you choose to do so, the matter will be dealt with differently. This matter will be finished when this conference is over and you have completed what people ask you to do to repair the harm. Is that clear?

4. Community Conference script

2. Telling the story

To the wrongdoer
..........., to help us understand what harm has been done and who has been affected by this incident, could you start by telling us what happened? How did you come to be involved? What were you thinking when you..........? What have you thought about since the incident? Who do you think has been affected by your actions? In what ways?

3. Exploring the harm

To the victim(s)
What did you think at the time? How has this incident affected you? What has been the worst of it for you?

To the victim supporters
What did you think when you heard about the incident? How do you feel about what has happened? What changes have you seen in (victims' names)? What has happened since?

To the wrongdoer supporters
This must be difficult for you to hear this. What did you think when you heard? How do you feel about what has happened? How are things between you all in the wake of what's happened?

4. Community Conference script

4. Acknowledgement and apology

To the wrongdoer

Now that you've heard from everybody about how they've been affected by what you've done, is there anything you want to say to (the victim), or anyone else here that might begin to make things right?

5. Agreement

To the victim first and then the victim supporters

What do you want to see happen as a result of the conference/meeting today (or to repair the harm/feel safe again)?

To wrongdoer and wrongdoer supporters

Does that seem fair? Is there something you'd like to see happen that might help?

To all conference participants

Who will be responsible for supervising the terms of the agreement? Let me just summarise what you have agreed upon.

6. Closing the conference

I will now record the agreement that's been reached here. This will formally close the matter, subject to completion of the agreement. You will each be asked to sign it and you will be given a copy before you leave. Is there anything else anyone wants to say? While I write down the agreement, which I will ask you all to sign before you leave, please enjoy the refreshments we have provided for you. Thank you all for your help today in resolving this difficulty.

Websites and training

Margaret Thorsborne and Associates: **www.thorsborne.com.au**
David Vinegrad: **behaviourmatters@hotmail.com**
Youth Justice Board: **www.justice.gov.uk/about/yjb**
Transforming Conflict: **www.transformingconflict.org**
International Institute for Restorative Practices: **www.iirp.org**
Restorative Practices International: **www.rpiassn.org**

School Programmes Websites
Friendly Schools and Families (Child Health Promotion Research Unit):
http://chpru.ecu.edu.au
Mind Matters: A Whole School Approach to Dealing with Bullying and Harassment
www.mindmatters.edu.au

A trilogy of training manuals by M Thorsborne and D Vinegrad
1. **Restorative Practices in Schools: Rethinking Behaviour Management**, 2003
2. **Restorative Practices in Classrooms: Rethinking Behaviour Management**, 2004
3. **Restorative Practices and Bullying: Rethinking Behaviour Management**, 2005
To purchase copies (UK): **www.incentiveplus.co.uk**
To purchase copies (Aus; NZ): **www.inyahead.com.au**

Recommended reading

So much has been written about restorative justice and the psychological theory that explains its effectiveness that a beginner could be overwhelmed. What we recommend below is a starting point. Each of these will lead you elsewhere. Do read more. It will increase your understanding of the field and, ultimately, your practice.

Are Zero Tolerance Policies Effective in the Schools? An Evidentiary Review and Recommendations. A Report by the American Psychological Association Zero Tolerance Task Force.

Beyond Discipline: From Compliance to Community by A Kohn. ASCD publication, 2006

Calling the Circle – The First and Future Culture by C Baldwin. Bantam publications, 1994

Just Schools: A Whole School Approach to Restorative Justice by B Hopkins. Jessica Kingsley Publishers, 2004

The Little Book of Restorative Justice by Howard Zehr. Good Books, 2002

The Name of the Game is Shame by D L Nathanson. S Tomkins Institute *www.tomkins.org*

Parenting for a Peaceful World by Robin Grille. Longueville Media, 2005

Restorative Justice in Everyday Life: Beyond the Formal Rituals by T Wachtel. *www.iirp.org/library/anu.html*

Restorative Justice Online – www.restorativejustice.org '…an authoritative, credible, non-partisan resource of information on restorative justice.'

Restoring Safe School Communities: A Whole School Response to Bullying, Violence and Alienation by B Morrison. Federation Press, 2007

About the authors

Margaret Thorsborne

is the Managing Director of Margaret Thorsborne and Associates, a consultancy committed to increasing job satisfaction and productivity by improving workplace and community relationships. Margaret pioneered the use of the formal conference process in schools in Queensland in the mid 90's and has trained conference facilitators in education, police and justice sectors across Australia, NZ, Britain, USA and Canada. She is widely regarded as an international expert in the implementation of restorative practices across whole school communities. She can be contacted at: www.thorsborne.co.uk and www.thorsborne.com.au

David Vinegrad

is the Director of Behaviour Matters, a consultancy providing training and leadership in restorative practice across all educational sectors. He has trained teachers and administrators in Singapore and Australia and more recently in Japan and Brazil. David has expanded the application of RP to tackle cyber bullying and problems arising from social networking across a diverse range of school communities. As a teacher and counsellor working in a range of international schools, David applies restorative practice daily in his classroom. He can be contacted at: www.behaviourmatters.org.au and dave@behaviourmatters.org.au

Order form

Your details

Name _____

Position _____

School _____

Address _____

_____

_____

Telephone _____

Fax _____

E-mail _____

VAT No. (EC only) _____

Your Order Ref _____

Please send me:

		No. copies
Restorative Justice	Pocketbook	☐
_____	Pocketbook	☐
_____	Pocketbook	☐
_____	Pocketbook	☐

Order by Post

Teachers' Pocketbooks
Laurel House, Station Approach
Alresford, Hants. SO24 9JH UK

Order by Phone, Fax or Internet

Telephone: +44 (0)1962 735573
Facsimile: +44 (0)1962 733637
Email: sales@teacherspocketbooks.co.uk
Web: www.teacherspocketbooks.co.uk

Customers in USA should contact:

2427 Bond Street, University Park, IL 60466
Tel: 866 620 6944 Facsimile: 708 534 7803
Email: mp.orders@ware-pak.com
Web: www.managementpocketbooks.com